The
Feel
Of
The
Sun

The
Feel
Of
The
Sun

POEMS BY

Mark Perlberg

Swallow Press   Ohio University Press
Chicago   Athens, Ohio   London

The author wishes to thank the editors of the following magazines, in which the following poems appeared: *The Hudson Review*: The Garden, Lines for Some Landscapes of the Northern Sung, A Northern Beach, There are Afternoons in Summer, View of Amsterdam, The Leap; *Poetry*: The Dead Fox, When At Night; *The American Scholar*: Baking Out; *The Nation*: Watercolor, April; *The New York Times*: This Bird of Georges Braque; *The Carleton Miscellany*: Summer Storm in Wisconsin, A Night Too Hot to Sleep; *Chicago Review*: To T'ao Ch'ien From Vinalhaven, Maine; *Focus/Midwest*: An Officer's Tartar Horse, Early One Morning; *Overtures*: The Bewitched Mill, The Inn, Casco Voyage; *Heartland II*, Northern Illinois University Press: Water and Light, Light and Water, Praise for Lichen; *Chicago Tribune Magazine*: From Another Country.

The Elegant Women and I Spend the Night in a Room by the River appeared in slightly different form in *Sunflower Splendor: Three Thousand Years of Chinese Poetry*, © Wu-Chi Liu and Irving Lo, Doubleday & Company; To the Tune, "Ku Yen Erh," *Inscape*.

Swallow Press Books
are published by
Ohio University Press
Athens, Ohio 45701

Library of Congress Cataloging in Publication Data

Perlberg, Mark, 1929-
    The feel of the sun.

    Part 4 consists of the author's translations of
selected poems by Tu Fu, Wang Wei, and Li Ch'ing-chao.
        I. Title.
PS3566.E6915F4   811'.54   81-8621
ISBN 0-8040-0422-6   AACR2
ISBN 0-8040-0423-4 (pbk.)

For Anna, and for Kate and Julie

Contents

I

The Garden

In memory of my mother

For weeks you had been journeying into yourself,
Slowly at first, and writing occasional poems
To mark certain junctions, dark and airy crossings.
Then as the illness gathered
And you began to shrink before our eyes,
Like a figure disappearing in space,
Your flight became a kind of inward freefall.
The last station you came to before the end was fear,

Fear so insistent that in your hospital room
Above the city, now remote as Arcturus,
You lay in a white silence, entirely alone—the living
    who came to you refused to countenance your journey—
Your face drawn about the bone, eyes uprolled, mouth gone,
Contracted on a single point of terror.

It was your daughter who loosed you from that mooring
By naming names:
Out of her own teeming conversations with herself
She knew that one must agree to meet with the dying,
    under a favorite tree, out on the edge of town,
    in front of a rain-streaked shop,
And walk part way with them, touching hands.
At last you had found a pilot for your journey.
It was a dusky afternoon in deep August.
Shadows of leaves stirred on the walls of the room.

She told you, now an unfamiliar, small old lady,
That she knew you would be able to do it,
And she returned bright fables learned from you as a child.
She said it is like the seasons following one another,
She talked of seeds sailing,
Of how the tall trees burn,
Of swallows blowing about in a gusty sky.

1

She said there would be a garden
Bright with so many flowers, with walks and grasses.
And your eyes widened at last before the end.
The great fear left you,
You grew easy in your pillows
And stepped light as a girl
Into the banks of shadows
That now drowned the walls of the room.

When At Night

My father sleeps in the sun porch
on a strange white bed.
I know what *gestorben* means.
Nobody said.

One day my father picked me up.
Ach du lieber Augustin, he sang, he sang.
Around, around the living room,
the big house rang.

He loves my sister more.
Sister's small and fat.
When I grow up I'll be like him—
gold mustache and a straw hat.

What does dying mean?
Is it living like a stone?
Being everywhere at once,
like river mist or rain?

Mama cries and cries.
She's wearing out her eyes.
Be a big boy, a good boy.
I don't cry.

In Mr. Gumbie's yard
the trees are clipped and strange;
the branches wrapped in gunny sacks
like bandaged hands.

Gumbie's in a box.
I saw, across the way.
They put the lid on.
They took him in the rain.

His face was brown as leaves.
He was bent and sick,
inching past my window,
loose coat, tapping stick.

I dream about my father.
Wind and cold rain.
He doesn't have a face.
The wind blew away his name.

Lines For Some Landscapes of the Northern Sung

Walk on beside your oxen, atom of a man.
Can you hear the water threading the brown cliffs high and
  away?
It plunges down the mountain into cloud,
  doubtless the source of the amber stream at your feet.
We are on a journey, you and I.
Perhaps you will lodge tonight at the inn that casts no shadows,
  across the stream, and then proceed refreshed
To the dark temple whose peaks break through the crab-claw
  trees
Beyond the bridge,
Seeing only the next turn of the tricky path.
But I can set my spirit soaring like the wind, like a ninth
  Immortal,
Everywhere at once in Fan K'uan's mountains.
I can leap the cliff's sheer, listen for the wind moaning
  in the gorges—was that a gibbon's scream?—
Float like mist in and about all the hollows,
While you clip-clop on, following your nose.
Never mind, we are both pilgrims in these tea-colored
  mountains
That pile into the crisp air with such vast solidity,
You by inheritance, I by hankering.
They tell us our place. They say something
Is solid as a planet in this heaving world.
And they say, perhaps, with T'ao Ch'ien,
That when the time comes for us to go into the mountains—
Do not make a fuss,
Step out quietly on the stream,
For the wind that blows against these peaks,
That shakes against the stars above the mountains,
Moves in your blood, and you and I are shadow and star.

Baking Out

Peaks Island, Maine

Old fellow, taking your ease by the hour in the sun
At the side of the clapboard house that faced the sea—
"Baking out," you called it, and you sat still in the sun
Half a day it seemed, head thrown back, eyes closed, smiling.
"My God, Harry, you're turning purple.
How can he sit so long in such a sun? Did anybody ever
see the like?" Mother was annoyed.
Such *sitzfleisch* made her angry.
"Where's Harry?"
"Where else? Baking out in the everlasting sun."
And on he sat in the summers turning dark
As the sun blazed its way across the sky.

What did he think about in the high hot sun of noon
And afternoon? I never thought to wonder—arrowing
Off on errands of my own. But I wonder now:
Did he dream in the pummeling sun?
Did he listen as I do now (eyes closed, head thrown back)
For the rustle of wind like water foaming
High in the trees across the road,
For the scrape of bayberry in a great green clump near his chair,
To the noise of kids calling, of gulls cackling, heckling, cawing?
Did this random mesh of sounds please him?
—Far from the East Side streets he knew as a boy,
Far from the pummeling gangs.

"—Irish and Italians they were. They'd clobber you
if you left your territory and crossed into theirs.
(He recounted the threat with zest.)
I was short but could run like sixty.
Did I tell you the time I won a medal in track?
I was a city kid in a camp in the mountains.
I ran the hundred without track shoes. Track shoes?
Whoever heard of track shoes?"

6

It was the one glory exploit of his youth
I knew about. And the time, in a boys' club,
He sang in *The Mikado*.
"On a tree by a willow . . . ," accompanying himself
With fluting whistlings.

Did the scent of weed on the beach,
The minty breath of the fields please him,
As he purpled like an Indian in the sun?
What of the sight of boats puttering, sailing, passing
On the endless lilting sea.
Of birds hunting, drifting on rivers of air?

Mostly, it was the feel of the sun, I think,
My stepfather loved,
Oiling the skin of the long dead boy,
Pouring some kind of honey.
Maybe he stored it up in his chair on the lawn
So it would glow in him all winter,
Through the fights, the arguments, the long subway rides,
The gray afternoons in the courthouse in the Bronx.

Old Harry, I hope that baking out
Was your time to dream
Long waking dreams bright as sails
In the late afternoon of your life,
Dreams you let no one enter,
As you sat on your rented lawn
By the sea and the Maine islands
In the light of the man-eating sun.

The Leap

My family moved to Kansas when I was a girl.
Father was an engineer and worked on a project there.
We lived in a house beyond the edge of town;
It stood by itself at the foot of a long, sloping hill.
Mother was strict. Every afternoon, even in summer,
She'd come to where I would be playing alone
And say, "Lou-Ann, go upstairs now and take your nap. It's
    time."
So, after a time I'd drag off with my doll to my room
Near the attic; it looked out over the wide empty fields.
Well, summers in Kansas are just not to be borne.
The heat goes over a hundred in the fields
And in any room in a house where the sun falls.
I was just a child; I couldn't stay on my bed,
    it got so warm.
I would lie on the floor with a cool patch of boards
Against my back, and smell the dust in my room,
And listen for the heat crackling in the empty fields.
Then, after a while, I'd get up and look out my window—
    way up the hill. And every afternoon at three
She'd come. Oh, it wasn't my mother.
A lady would ride up the hill on a great white horse.
She was dressed in white, always.
She'd rein in her horse at the brow of the hill
And stand there, looking.
Then she'd leap—horse and all—into the river.
I learned to wait for her ride in that sullen heat,
Every day at three in the afternoon,
And for her long silent fall to the water.

I kept that story to myself for thirty years.
Then one day I told mother.
"Lou-Ann," she said, "I'm amazed.
You know there wasn't a river near our house.
The nearest was twenty miles away."
"Is that so," I said. "Isn't it strange, then,
that I learned to wait for the woman and her white horse,
that I counted on their coming,
and their leap together—their long floating fall to the river—
all those summer afternoons,
in the heat, in my room,
in the house in Kansas."

Lonesomest Sound

What if all the sounds ever made
do not dissipate in space
but travel on and on like light from a star.
Somewhere over the land, the *whoo-whoo-ee*
of a scrapped diesel train. Lonesomest sound.
You who are old as I will hear it again,
hoarse above dream fields.

This Bird of Georges Braque

For S. Ronald Weiner (1933-1969)

This bird of Georges Braque
This arrangement of planes
Hangs in an unseen warp of space
It skims chill pinnacles of sky
Its wings shadow sleep's meadows
It is a white sail moving
Beyond day beyond evening

To T'ao Ch'ien From Vinalhaven, Maine

What would my old friend say of this prospect,
who, from a bird's homeward flight,
from the sight of sun lingering on Southern Mountain,
"almost learned the truth."

You are beside me here, T'ao Ch'ien.
Tell me, what do you think of the mist
erasing that jagged row of pines
descending the slope to the bay?
Does not the scene recall a Chinese painting?
I think you'd admire the road, the green, the snail
glistening with wet,
and berries—drops of blood-red jade—
just off the path in the woods,
and scent of mint and dogrose blowing.

Today I climbed the hill to the island graveyard
and lay in the grass to read
the lichen-spotted stones.
One took my heart, Old Ghost,
not twelve inches high—"Lottie,
dau. of G. & A. F. Young, born 1883,"
dead nine years later.
"This is a little grave, but O, have a care,
For world-wide hopes lie buried here.
How much light, how much joy
Lies buried with our darling girl."
Lilies and the morning glory—carved
in the sea-gray stone.

Master, let us converse and make what we can
of all these things.
We'll meet at the eastern hedge.
Let me bring the wine you were so fond of.

II

Summer Storm In Wisconsin

Thunder woke us early
In the cabin under the trees.
It was dawn, gray and watery—
Then the light grew green as under sea.
More lightning, sudden rain.
Then the fume of cedar on the breeze.

Water and Light, Light and Water

1

At the lake's edge
In an inch of water
Minnows move above sand ridges
Stroked by loops, by nets of light.

2

The late sun hangs over the lake's rim.
Rings of light, shaken from the water,
Climb the cedars.
Along the broken pier the clear light
Sings in the thistles.

A Night Too Hot to Sleep

One night long ago
On a night as dank as this,
My father came to our room.
"How would you and Sis
Like to go out for a ride?
It's much too hot to sleep."

I recall my sister's face
Upturned to greet his
As he carried us downstairs,
How her hair bobbed up and down,
And the ribbon in her hair.
And even the shift she wore,
Dotted with little bears.

We stepped out into the night
Out of the square of light
That fell from the front door
And got in the big car
And rode around the town
With our father.

So great a treat it was,
So rare a treat it was,
It lingers with me still:
The three of us in the car
Tooling around the town
On a night too hot to sleep.

My father was soon dead.
Of his few nights with us,
This is the one I keep.

The Revenant

I came, a stranger, an intruder.
I arrived from long ago
and on a fur-soft summer night
parked my car in tall shadows
that half-hid the house my father built.
It rose in the darkness, still commanding the street
at the head of the hill where the cliffs and the river meet.

A young man came down the slate walk
where I played as a child,
when June evenings were stitched with fireflies.
He stood outside the hedges.
"Can I help you, sir?"
"Thank you," I said. "No—but I used to live here once."
"Oh," he said, then turned and walked briskly into the dark.
No ghosts for him this evening.

I might have said, but had sought to spare us both,
that my father, when he was younger than I am now,
had built this house, and died suddenly after,
on the porch that faces south.

What had I hoped to find in this mute return—
that my unknown parent had inherited his house in death?
That he was the true tenant, still there
in the shrubs, the garden, the insubstantial air;
did I expect to hear his laugh, to feel his hand upon my hair?

Who now was the ghost, my father or myself,
who like a stone fallen out of space,
had struck across the orbit of this young man,
raising I cannot know what dust
in the cliffs and precipices of his mind.

From Another Country

The children have gone, leaving their round signs
And hieroglyphs—fragments of the language of their country—
Chalked on this darkening asphalt edge of the park.
They have set down numbers, carefully, in a ring
(Some are written backwards). And they have drawn dreamy
    girls,
Each with a crescent smile and bouncy hair,
And crowned each head with a bow. The park is silent;
A leaf floats down to the chalky center of the scene.
But what matters is no longer in the picture:
The artists have scattered to their suppers and their baths,
Leaving in the hour's tranquil light a sense of emptiness.
It is clear that those who worked with such seriousness here
Were girls, but there is no hint of their individual lives,
For all the chalky drawings are the same.
So childhood was a gate through which we came.
Pharoah's children, too, must have sketched
Just such marvelous matters upon perishable walls.

Seven Children: On a Photograph From Vietnam

My daughters started home on a summer day
as clouds, blue with electricity, piled in the sky
and drops began to smack against the street.
When they turned the corner, lightning raveled the air,
thunder cracked, wind, rain lashed them.
Down the street they raced, screaming,
and fell in the door out of the storm,
wet as if they had been lifted by their mother
out of the tub, accusing.
Where was father when the sky broke,
who had met them only at the door?
Pieces of that day still flicker in their dreams.

Now come five small children of Vietnam
running out of a photo in the news.
The white-shirted boy nearest bitterly shrieks/cries: fear
lives in his face.
A girl in the center, naked, holds out her arms,
hands dangling (as though flicking off bath water;
as though to be lifted by someone from the tub).
The jellied fire eats her narrow back.
An older girl bumps along the road
with a small boy. They hold hands, running.
And the littlest stops and looks behind him.
They are fleeing storms of fire, of tiger-roar/lion-roar,
of dragon crash and bellow.
What of their dreams, after the flesh of the burned girl
has stopped melting like wax into the napalm?
Father, whom will they accuse?

Graffiti

*The most important part of Spaceship Earth: the instruction
booklet that didn't come with the package.*

*

Everybody wants to go to heaven but nobody wants to die.

*

—Lincoln Park, Chicago

How to put it briefer, better—
the cosmic grumble: I ache, therefore I am?
Your sayings, nameless calligraphers,
penny metaphysicians,
painted on rocks at the lake's edge
in colors that shine in rain!

Ghost Dog

Somewhere, back of my house,
in the night, in the snow, a dog howling.
I think it's a dog; it ought to be night,
but the shadow of smoke blows across
the brick back of the house opposite.
And shadows of trees.

The howl again. Has someone left a dog
tied up in all this cold? The sound deepens.
It has arrived from a great distance, like starlight.
It moves low, just audible now, winding, curling
along the ground.
A wolf, head upraised, leg mashed in a trap,
under the arrows of the Northern Lights?
One who has come back, baffled, nattering,
mourning some wrong, unknowable as a rune?

Wind across a col at the bottom of my mind.

The Dance

Your heart's mottled darkness.
It is the flower of your wound
that sets her clacking, rocking, maundering
in a fever of rage and shame.
Crookback dancers in spidery *pas de deux*.
Principals in a nether idyll.

The Cage

Rage, dark and scarab-secret
flares in you like lightning in a tomb,
rending your days,
hauling into the shoals of sleep
woundflowers of dream.

The Time is Near

The time is near, despite the delicate plants
you nurture in your window,
when you will turn to stone.
True, there is blood in your victim's stool;
he dizzies at the thrusts, the mountain silences.
Yes, his heart is acid; soon he'll fall on the stairs,
but your eyes are onyx,
your nails will slide into iron,
and you will pace back and forth in your room
willing pain,
vacant as an Aztec god of war.

Reflection

Hands in a night window
I thought meant harm—
my own.

The Dead Fox

Suddenly, on the asphalt road,
struck by a car,
lying in his own bright blood—
night messenger,
dark star of the wood.

The Inn

After traveling for days we came to an inn. At first we were unaware of its great size because we arrived at night and mist was swirling. We took rooms in a kind of Victorian turret, but in the morning, when we walked outside to explore the grounds, we found that there was no end to the inn. Its towers, walls seemed to spread everywhere. We walked all morning through wet grass and never came to the end of the place. It was maddening. The world was suddenly like a photograph completely filled up with this inn, and oddest of all, the place didn't even have a name.

Lamed Vav

And will they seem strange when they appear to us,
dusty, horny-handed, muttering dark prayers?

Come forward, precious ones.
Leave your houses of study, your little groceries,
where neon Stars of David sizzle and burn in the windows,
where the Orthodox troop to buy their white soap
veined with blue calligraphy of Hebrew,
and the candles that leap and throb for the dead.
Leave your dim tailor shops,
let the doors of your *shuls* hang open.
Come from your cracked schoolrooms.
Show us your faces.

III

View of Amsterdam

an etching by Rembrandt

Tranquility of a spring or summer day.
Water is running in the marshes.
The sky is cloudless. All is distantly seen.
Two small figures, blotches, barely, walk upon a thread of road,
Beyond which a line of low buildings faces the harbor.
Above them, bigger than the church, a windmill—
    bold cross of commerce—is scratched against the sky,
And others run in a faint file to the horizon.
Beyond the salt marsh and a stretch of harbor water,
Vessels at dockside. Not a smoke wisp curls in the air.
It must be morning.

Sunday

Imogene Cunningham took a photograph
Of an unmade bed.
Who would have thought of it?
A few whorls and folds of sheets,
A comb and hairpins.
Who would have thought of . . .
Of Aphrodite poised upon her shell
Of tortoises and combs of honey
Of slow-moving sunny Sunday mornings,
With leaves scraping against the brick outside.

The Moment

From the painting, "The Mother,"
by Pieter de Hooch

Before the umber curtains in the dusky room
she begins to unlace her bodice, which is crimson.
It is a morning at the end of winter.
Light clear as the ice at the edge of the canals
lacquers the frame of the upper casement windows,
pinks against a copper warming pan, glazes the floor,
tiled black and white like a chess board.

A sound she made—the scrape of her shoe?—
startled the small sleeping dog.
Up on all fours, backside to viewer,
it glares at her, while she,
a slant smile beginning,
turns to the child in the hooded wicker cradle.
We do not see its face.

In the hall, a girl of four or five,
in cap, rough floor-length smock and apron,
stands at a half-opened door,
gazes into the morning.
Light angles into the hall, kindles a side of the door frame,
ignites a yellow patch along the wall.
For the moment, nothing vibrates with sound.
The grammar of the scene is present tense.
But the dog will drop with a rasp of breath
to resume his doze.
The child will smack, will suck at the breast,
the girl turn, or hum, or crash
out into the morning.
The tense will shift: future, past, past perfect.

The Bewitched Mill

A painting by Franz Marc

Water falls upon the great wheel,
and at the gathering pool beneath the mill
blue animals drink.
And birds on branches flash and sing
in the arch of falling water.

Some beasts have come to drink
that they may never die;
others to be whole again.
But some move out of the woods
toward the rumor of the dusky waters
so they will not forget, down the fall of years,
the possibility of exultation.

Fireworks

There was wind high in the dark
Blowing through the trees with the surf's sound,
Making large upper branches rock and creak,
And smoky clouds that rolled the moon around,
And the rich, rising scent of a birchlog fire.

Then: runs, bursts, scatterings of children's laughter
Outside on the grounds that tore in the wind
And flew in the night like the zig-zag sparks
That fountained from a dozen Fourth of July wands
The kids had found somewhere on the place, and—
　　chasing, shouting, running, stumbling, calling!

The Father of Emily Dickinson Rings the Church Bells in Amherst, Massachusetts

Edward Dickinson, attorney,
treasurer of Amherst College,
prompt in all his comings and goings—his
    newspaper must be placed just so, under
    the lamp, at his chair—
iron forged in the New England furnace,
Emily's most demanding love,
banged shut his front door on a winter night,
rushed to the tall church on Carver Street,
and gulping down the icy air,
rang rang rang all the bells.

Townsmen heard the bells cry *fire*.
They ran into the streets at the signal.
But it was only Emily's father, hatless, in frock coat,
ringing in the frozen passion of the Northern Lights
that shook cold silk against the stars.

The Master

Near the edge of a town on the River Wei,
where a few scattered huts climbed the back of the mountain,
lived one so schooled in the *tao* of painting,
his curling dragons flapped off walls.
They raced storm clouds and entered
the watery life of streams.
Near Ch'ang-an was another: a silk wind moved
    in his bamboo groves.
Spring, like memory, stirred in a room
where his pictures hung.
But what do you make of the master of masters
(he was seen at odd hours on the streets of the capital)
who, tiring of the world of men,
painted a cave and disappeared inside.

A Ming Dynasty Kuan Yin *

The Art Institute of Chicago

She dreams of the hissings that suns make,
is warmed by fires that drive remotest stars.

* Buddhist goddess of mercy

Poet to Poet

I know a poet—he wears dark glasses always,
even after nightfall.
His advice, a mountain-man's knowledge,
delivered in soft West Virginian:
"Don't let the bastards get a bead on ya."
Which I take to mean,
be elusive, like the quicksilver rain,
be sudden as ground fog, and scary,
be not straight or plain; be hidden,
take the sly cat for totem.
Be nobody's pet.
Make Hermes your guide, patron of thieves,
winged wayfarer god with a fondness
for bent ways, for crossroads.
Be secret as a spy, various, patient,
and you'll get by.

Watercolor: April

Violet, coral, lemon.
The tissues of the flowering trees
streak the wind.

You Will Know

You will know it is time
when you arrive at an unknown shore
and all appears familiar.
You are indifferent to curious beach stones—
their shapes and colors—
to the tilt of summer fields,
how the trout hang in pools like dark flags.
You sense that soon you will be part
of all these things,
and of the lip of a falling wave,
of sunlight in leaves, leaf-shadow, the leaves themselves.
You hear your voice in the high sweet notes
of the phoebe's call.

The Yellow Door

The sun, for a moment this late February afternoon,
has dropped between a row of crumbling buildings
at the alley's end, blazing
into my study, throwing silky shadows
of table, books and drooping asparagus fern
on the yellow door—and prickly cactus,
which, as the punctual sun of winter flames and passes
dreams of Texas or of Jalisco's yellow sands.

Welcome

I step from my house in the deep city
surprised by the odor of lilac—
sudden as a slap, as an unexpected caress.
My lilacs, almost trees, touching windows,
billowing against the brick.
Up the street, the odor of lilac,
coasting casual gasoline smells.
And beyond—traces, vivid as color.
—Father, you who went over so long ago,
could you visit your son, now,
now might be the time.

IV

Jade Flower Palace

by Tu Fu

Where the stream turns and wind rises in the pines,
Gray mice scatter over fallen roof tiles.
I do not know what prince built this palace
In a cliff's shelter, or why it became a forgotten ruin.
Near the path eroded by the stream,
Green ghost fires flicker in dark rooms.
Ten thousand sounds float from unseen flutes,
As autumn color scatters again from the trees.
The prince's pliant girls lie in their yellow graves—
One thinks of their trailing silks and scents,
Of their brows blackened for beauty.
Only a stone horse, among the old things,
Waits for the gold carriages.
Grief seizes me and I fall to the grass.
Filled with lamentation I weep and sing.
As we make our way in the world,
Who can say what waits for us?

An Officer's Tartar Horse

by Tu Fu

This is one of the Tartar horses of Ferghana.
Note its great frame, so lean, so angular.
Its ears rise up like pointed bamboo shoots.
Its hoofs are light as wind.
To a beast with such esprit
I could trust my life. With such a horse,
For whom ten thousand miles is a morning gallop,
I could face eternity.

I Spend the Night in a Room by the River

by Tu Fu

Darkness still shadows the mountain road
As I gaze from my study above the watergate.
Streamers of cloud rest on the brow of a cliff,
While the orphan moon tumbles among the waves.
A line of cranes winds overhead in silent flight.
Below, a pack of wolves quarrels over food.
Grieved by the war, I have not slept.
Who has the strength to right heaven and earth?

The Elegant Women

by Tu Fu

On the third day of the third month, in fresh weather,
The elegant women of the capital stroll on the riverbank,
Their manner regal and remote, their faces delicate,
Their figures shapely and pleasing.
Wrapped in filmy silks bright with peacocks and silver unicorns,
They illumine the spring evening.
What do they wear in their hair?
The hummingbird headdress with jade leaves dangling
Past their lips.
What do you see upon their shoulders?
Capes with crushed pearls at their waists that cling
To their bodies.
One even glimpses from time to time,
Glittering beneath the canopies of the empresses' pavilion,
Those great ladies of the empire, Kuo and Ch'in.

Purple steak from the camel's hump broiled in a glistening pan
And the white flesh of fish are set out in rows of crystal dishes.
But the great ones ignore the elegant table
And all the meats minced into silk-fine shreds.
Yet still the palace eunuchs arrive.
They rein in their horses without so much as stirring dust,
And set before the guests food rare as jewels
Brought from the eight corners of the earth.
The music of pipes and drums, strange enough to move the dead,
Accompanies the feast.
                              Now the latecomer arrives.
He dismounts and enters behind the silk curtains,
As willow seed snows down upon green duckweed,
And a bluebird flies off with a scarlet kerchief in his beak.
Be careful! So great is his power his lightest touch can burn.
Do not approach too close to the prime minister.
He may be angry.

To the Tune, "Ku Yen Erh"

by Li Ch'ing-chao

Words do not serve.
I take up my pen but words are shadows.
I test myself. Can I write a few lines?

I know that before I tried to set down my
    feelings as words
They did not seem false to my ears.

Dawn. I rise from my bed and open the paper
    screen.
There are no words for my emptiness.
The jade burner is cold, the fume of the
    incense scattered.
All seems watery as my feelings.
Three notes remain locked within the flute
And the plum is frightened and shattered.
How many Aprils will find me sorrowing?
The small wind, the scattered rain, the
    grieving earth
Force a thousand tears from my eyes.
The one who played the flute is gone, his jade
    tower empty.
I feel nothing. Who will help me?
I cut a flower branch but there is no one
    to offer it to under heaven.

In the Mountains

by Wang Wei

White stones rise out of Thorn Creek.
Cold weather. Red leaves are few.
On the mountain path that has long been without rain,
Green mist dampens my clothing.

An Autumn Evening in the Mountains

by Wang Wei

A fresh rain in the empty mountains
Has brought with it the chill of autumn.
The clear stream flows over rocks and pebbles.
Water lilies shake beneath a passing fisherman's boat.
From the bamboo grove—the chatter of girls
    returning with their wash.
The fragrance of spring has run its course,
But you, old friend, stay with me a while.

V

Casco
Voyage

There Are Afternoons in Summer

There are afternoons in summer that are so fine
They seem an interval of time's first day that has never ended
And will never end.

I am sure it is the palpable force of the light,
Of light so clear that one sees everything open to air:
    the veins on the underside of leaves
    the sharp serrations of the fern
    the shadow cast by each small stone
    the glass edge of the sea that is the horizon's line
    the sun flinging diamond fires from a patch of the bay,
    the luminous wing-edge of a gull crossing.

The illusion dies as the day dies
When light lies down level in the weeds
And the sky in the west takes color like a bruise
And the evening walks in cold shadows like the morning.

Early One Morning

Until my walk this morning I had forgotten
that wind can be freighted with the scent of raspberries,

that things like ropes or an old pot on a porch
will creak in wind.

—A gull's shadow slides across the road,
ripples up the side of a house, and is gone.

A Northern Beach

Deer Isle, Maine

A beach on a northern island
Needs getting used to: there is so much to understand.
First there are the rocks that slide and roll underfoot—
Their shapes and tints and textures (do not expect much
    sand)—
Oval rocks, casually sought by strollers on an August morning,
As are the round stones; all shapes that fit the hand.
Tints catch the eye: the salt and pepper flecks of gray granite,
The creamy sheen of quartz, and those black stones
Veined by starry bursts and traceries that seem a chunk of space
    fallen from the sky.
There are the shales, with shades of violet, bronze
And lichen green. They make fine skipping stones.
Once I found a slab crossed by streams of garnets.
Flints and hunks of marble are waxen to the touch,
And there are rocks grained and weathered like driftwood;
Some glint with mica.
After the rocks, the seaweed,
Dark and leathery at the fringes that lift and fall in the clear
    tides,
The color of mustard on the humped part of the mounds
That have lain longer in the periodic sun.
Beyond the beach and the island's bedrock
That lies in flat, animal shapes back to the trees,
Are the trees themselves: the angular pine and fir and cedar,
Which may, perhaps like the beach, be just now slipping into
    fog.
Hold these elements (not forgetting the glint of the water
    with its colors dimming in the fog; the occasional small boat
    tugging at its mooring; the high, sweet sound of birds
    singing in the pines; the salt scent from sea and weeds;
    the peppermint wash from the meadows behind the trees),
Hold these elements: then mark how perspective changes
At the slightest turn of the light—or of the mind.

In Praise of Lichen

It lives on mere banks and drifts of air
And where nothing else will,
Growing in ashy moonbursts on bare boulders
    in the sun's brightest flare, beneath a shine of ice,
    in blowing salt air.
Its medallions color the bark of trees;
They seal gravestones—a glad sign
In the windy margins of the world, of increase
Near the domain of zero.

Bright Day on Lane Island

Small wind noises: puffs, hissings,
watery susurrations.
Tough plants erect in stony meadows:
raspberry, juniper, wildrose, goldenrod.
Old rock, gray-green, lichen-starred.
And pouring light everywhere flooding
this little island, the outer islands,
the great blue lyric sea.

Littoral

On our island
the rock you pick up
along the stony shore
changes in your hand
to fish, to cloud,
as cloud is dolphin, whale
and granite cliff,
now catching shifting light.
Down on the beach
the child that was you
fetches an oval stone
and under flaring sun,
with paint and brush,
transforms it to an image of herself,
Or you or me.

Once

I pull my car off the road
and walk toward the bass mutter of sea voices,
an inlander now, but shaped, imprinted
by the grave polyphony.
(Sun dried, wind burnished grass along the path's edge,
hissed in arthritic pines.)
Fierce light, warm rushing wind.
Below, in the cove: canon and fugue.
I rise, a hawk climbing air,
dwindle, a speck, arcing toward noon.

Things

Odor of hot bread
from the island bakery.
The summer house, *Sans Faux*;
porch in the shape of an L,
high over the rocky beach.
Mother's tale of a hundred seals;
they clambered out on that beach
in a night of wind and spray
under a rolling moon.
Breasts of our summer girl
surprised after a swim.
Nipples great as the largest coins.
The swim in the cold strait
to the fort on Cushing's Island:
Dim rows of artillery shells
in tunnels under the cliff,
each shell near as tall as I was.
The physician in his dark suit
in his office on Island Street.
His gloved wooden hand
resting on the sill in the sun.
My own sunbrowned feet,
on the rocks, grass, dirt paths.
The ice house off the road—
windowless, silvered wood.
It sagged in a patch of swamp
in striped, tigerish shade.
The cottage on Spar Cove.
Its stained mirrors that will see
none of us ever again.

Casco Voyage

The islands swam toward us out of the haze
in heat that cooked the deck of the bay steamer.
Their names were songs: Cushings & Hope & Basket;
Peaks, Chebeague, the Diamonds—the liquid disc of the sun
dropped behind Great Diamond's dock
throughout my boyhood summers—
Jewel, with its dark, abandoned watchtower, and Cliff Island,
both on the bay's outer rim. Beyond, over the sill
of the world: England.

I dreamed of such a ride when I was a boy,
combing my island's shores
for shells and colored stones
or fishing from rocks in green swells.
I'd have run away with anyone
who would have taken me down Casco Bay
toward the sea-blasts where the porpoise rolled.
But there were no takers.

So I returned at last, with children of my own,
paid cash at the Bay Line's window in Portland—splendid
the rush of smells: brine, engine oil, fish!
They named the place like a sign.
We sailed out with the tourists
that hottest day of the year.

We often rowed past Evergreen Landing
at the Island's tip—my brother, friends, and I—
to Pumpkin Knob. It poked its green hump
off Peak's northeast shore.
We'd tie up to a bouy and fish in the sun,
by the Knob's great single house,
its red roof timbers down,
its pier washed out in a forgotten winter storm.
Trees splashed shadow over cold panes.

Once we reached Long Island, a pair of us pulling
across bottomless Hussey Sound.
We raced on the white beach,
crashed into surf that washed a foreign island.
Sunlight shook in diamond waves
off the water.

The only breeze that stirred for twenty miles
we made ourselves, as we moved by
capes and twists, neck and knuckles of land—
Merriconeag, Harpswell, Little Johns,
Orrs Island. "Did you know," I heard my Mother say,
"Harriet Beecher Stowe had a house on Orrs Island?"

When the captain pulled the cord in the pilot house—
we stood in its strip of shade—I saw the old wood steamers
whose whistles hooted through my long summer days.

I pointed to every nook I knew about
in our part of the bay,
and from our guide that afternoon:
"Coming in view to port—Little Mark Island.
The stone tower near shore was a shelter built
by shipwrecked sailors.
Over to starboard, that's Eagle Island.
The lone house that looks like a ship
was built by Admiral Peary, after . . ."

When we made the turn and steamed
back toward Portland,
I knew I had traveled toward this ride for twenty years,
not just to glimpse far-off beaches, mythical cliffs,
the still steep-sided coves,
but to seize that glistening land
where a part of me was born.

There's Mother on the porch at Hadlock's Cove:
young, brisk, ironic—splitting the air with a whistle,
hauling in her errant boys.
(I forgive you my dear dead Mother,
as I know you had forgiven me.
Measureless the distances on the wind-streaked summer sea.)
There's Frank Finnerty: His great black lobster boat
stinks like a garbage scow.
He smiles without any bottom teeth.
And his wife with flecked, hazel eyes; her laugh
rings like a kettle banged with a ladle.
And my girl with lilting breasts
and mouth soft as air.
There—crisscrossing gleams of the night boats
and voices over the water,
and sweeping Ram Island Light: it brushed the walls
of my room, punctual, scary,
nightlong in the dark of a flying summer.

Notes on the Translations

TU FU (712-770) and Wang Wei (698-759) were poets of T'ang dynasty (618-907) China. Wang Wei was also a painter and is traditionally considered the father of Chinese landscape painting, although none of his paintings have come down to us. A great Sung poet said that his poems were like paintings and his painting was like poetry.

Tu Fu was a master of the highly complex verse forms of his age and wrote with great depth of feeling and an often powerful density of language. In "The Elegant Women," he guardedly satirizes the luxury of the T'ang court, soon to be torn by a rebellion that eventually destroyed the dynasty.

Li Ch'ing-chao (1081-1149) lived during the Sung (960-1280). All her verse is love poetry. Its delicate and complex tone grows darker as she endures prolonged separations from her husband, a scholar-official of the government. After his early death the note is darker still, the verse increasingly more complex. She wrote in the *t'zu* form, in which poets wrote their own words to popular songs of the day. Because the song titles bear no resemblance to the poetry, they are usually not translated, as is the case here.